MR. BOUNCE

by Roger Hargreaves

Mr Bounce was very small and like a rubber ball.

He just couldn't keep himself on the ground!

He bounced all over the place!

And, as you can imagine, that made things rather difficult.

Last week, for instance, Mr Bounce was out walking when he came to a farm.

He climbed over the farm gate, and you can guess what happened next, can't you?

He jumped down from the gate, and . . .

. . . bounced right into the duckpond!

BOUNCE went Mr Bounce.

SPLASH went Mr Bounce.

"QUACK," went the ducks.

The other morning, for instance, Mr Bounce was in bed.

He woke up, and jumped out of bed, and you can guess what happened next, can't you?

He bounced right out of his bedroom door and all the way downstairs.

Bouncebouncebouncebounce!

That happens quite often, which probably explains why Mr Bounce leaves his bedroom door open every night!

After he had picked himself up Mr Bounce went inside his house and sat down to think.

BOUNCE.

Mr Bounce bounced off the chair and banged his head on the ceiling.

BANG went Mr Bounce's head on the ceiling.

"OUCH!" said Mr Bounce.

"This is ridiculous," Mr Bounce thought to himself, rubbing his head. "I must do something to stop all this bouncing about."

He thought and thought.

"I know," he thought. "I'll go and see the doctor!"

So, after breakfast, Mr Bounce set off to the nearest town to see the doctor.

He was passing a tennis court when he tripped over a pebble.

BOUNCE he bounced.

And he bounced right on to the court where two children were playing tennis, and you can guess what happened next, can't you?

The children didn't realise that Mr Bounce wasn't a tennis ball, and started hitting him with their tennis racquets backwards and forwards over the net.

BOUNCE!

"OOO!"

BOUNCE!

"OW!"

BOUNCE!

"OUCH!"

Poor Mr Bounce.

Eventually, one of the children hit Mr Bounce so hard he bounced right out of the tennis court.

Mr Bounce bounced off down the road towards the town.

"Oh dear," he said, feeling very sorry for himself. "I've been bounced black and blue!"

A bus was coming down the road, and Mr Bounce decided that the safest place for him to be would be to be on it.

He got on and sat down, still feeling more than a little sorry for himself.

The bus drove into town.

The bus stopped right outside the doctor's.

Mr Bounce stepped down from the bus.

And you can guess what happened next, can't you?

He didn't step down on to the pavement outside the doctor's. Oh no, not Mr Bounce!

He stepped off the bus, and on to the pavement, and bounced, in through the doctor's window!

Dr Makeyouwell was sitting at his desk, enjoying his mid-morning cup of coffee.

Mr Bounce sailed through the open window, and landed . . .

Well, you can guess where he landed, can't you?

That's right!

SPLASH went the coffee.

"OUCH!" squeaked Mr Bounce. The coffee was rather hot.

"Good heavens," exclaimed Dr Makeyouwell.

After the doctor had fished Mr Bounce out of his coffee, and sat him on some blotting paper to dry out, he listened to what Mr Bounce had to tell him.

"So you see," said Mr Bounce finally, "you must give me something to stop me bouncing about all over the place quite so much."

"Hmmm," pondered the doctor.

After some thought Dr Makeyouwell went to his medicine cabinet and took out a pair of tiny red boots.

"This should do the trick," he told Mr Bounce. "Heavy boots! That should stop the bouncing!"

"Oh, thank you, Dr Makeyouwell," said Mr Bounce and walked home wearing his red boots.

Not bounced!

Walked!

· That night Mr Bounce went to bed wearing his heavy boots.

And then he went to sleep.

The following morning, he woke up and yawned and stretched, and bounced out of bed.

And can you guess what happened next?

No, he didn't bounce down the stairs.

He went straight through the bedroom floorboards,

and finished up in the kitchen!

3 Great Offers for MR. MEN Fans!

MR. MEN TOKEN

1 New Mr. Men or Little Miss Library Bus Presentation Cases

A brand new stronger, roomier school bus library box, with sturdy carrying handle and stay-closed fasteners.

The full colour, wipe-clean boxes make a great home for your full collection.

They're just £5.99 inc P&P and free bookmark!

☐ MR. MEN ☐ LITTLE MISS (please tick and order overleaf)

2 Door Hangers and Posters

PLEASE STICK YOUR 50P COIN HERE

In every Mr. Men and Little Miss book like this one, you will find a special token. Collect 6 tokens and we will send you a brilliant Mr. Men or Little Miss poster and a Mr. Men or Little Miss double sided full colour bedroom door hanger of your choice. Simply tick your choice in the list and tape a 50p coin for your two items to this page.

Door Hangers (please tick)
☐ Mr. Nosey & Mr. Muddle
☐ Mr. Slow & Mr. Busy
☐ Mr. Messy & Mr. Quiet
☐ Mr. Perfect & Mr. Forgetful
☐ Little Miss Fun & Little Miss Late
☐ Little Miss Helpful & Little Miss Tidy
☐ Little Miss Busy & Little Miss Brainy
☐ Little Miss Star & Little Miss Fun

Posters (please tick)
☐ MR.MEN
☐ LITTLE MISS

3 Sixteen Beautiful Fridge Magnets – any 2 for £2.00!
inc.P&P

They're very special collector's items!
Simply tick your first and second* choices from the list below
of any 2 characters!

1st Choice
- [ ] Mr. Happy
- [ ] Mr. Lazy
- [ ] Mr. Topsy-Turvy
- [ ] Mr. Bounce
- [ ] Mr. Bump
- [ ] Mr. Small
- [ ] Mr. Snow
- [ ] Mr. Wrong
- [ ] Mr. Daydream
- [ ] Mr. Tickle
- [ ] Mr. Greedy
- [ ] Mr. Funny
- [ ] Little Miss Giggles
- [ ] Little Miss Splendid
- [ ] Little Miss Naughty
- [ ] Little Miss Sunshine

2nd Choice
- [ ] Mr. Happy
- [ ] Mr. Lazy
- [ ] Mr. Topsy-Turvy
- [ ] Mr. Bounce
- [ ] Mr. Bump
- [ ] Mr. Small
- [ ] Mr. Snow
- [ ] Mr. Wrong
- [ ] Mr. Daydream
- [ ] Mr. Tickle
- [ ] Mr. Greedy
- [ ] Mr. Funny
- [ ] Little Miss Giggles
- [ ] Little Miss Splendid
- [ ] Little Miss Naughty
- [ ] Little Miss Sunshine

*Only in case your first choice is out of stock.

CUT ALONG DOTTED LINE AND RETURN THIS WHOLE PAGE

TO BE COMPLETED BY AN ADULT

To apply for any of these great offers, ask an adult to complete the coupon below and send it with the appropriate payment and tokens, if needed, to MR. MEN OFFERS, PO BOX 7, MANCHESTER M19 2HD

- [ ] Please send _____ Mr. Men Library case(s) and/or _____ Little Miss Library case(s) at £5.99 each inc P&P
- [ ] Please send a poster and door hanger as selected overleaf. I enclose six tokens plus a 50p coin for P&P
- [ ] Please send me _____ pair(s) of Mr. Men/Little Miss fridge magnets, as selected above at £2.00 inc P&P

Fan's Name _____

Address _____

_____ **Postcode** _____

Date of Birth _____

Name of Parent/Guardian _____

Total amount enclosed £ _____

- [ ] **I enclose a cheque/postal order payable to Egmont Books Limited**
- [ ] **Please charge my MasterCard/Visa/Amex/Switch or Delta account** (delete as appropriate)

| | | | | | | | | | | | | | | | | Card Number |

Expiry date ___/___   **Signature** _____

Please allow 28 days for delivery. We reserve the right to change the terms of this offer at any time but we offer a 14 day money back guarantee. This does not affect your statutory rights.

MR.MEN   LITTLE MISS
Mr. Men and Little Miss™ & ©Mrs. Roger Hargreaves